I CHOOSE
to Make Good Decisions

ELIZABETH
ESTRADA

I CHOOSE
to Make Good Decisions

I
CHOOSE
SERIES

ELIZABETH ESTRADA

Have you ever had to make a difficult decision?
Or has a tough problem ever faced you?
The kind of tricky issue where
You don't know what to do.

You want to make a good choice
That leaves you with pride,
But you're not quite sure which way to go,
Which way to decide?

Life is full of decisions,
Whether to tell the truth or a lie.
And even in a game that you're losing,
You decide to still try.

Maybe it's whether or not to keep working hard,
Or give up when it gets tough.
Good decisions are hard to make,
Especially when life gets rough.

Decisions come up in life,
Each and every day.
And sometimes, with decisions,
There is a right and a wrong way.

Some decisions are bigger than others.
The impact can leave others hurt.
The feeling you get when you make the wrong choice,
Well, to me, there is nothing worse.

When someone is feeling sad,
I use words that are kind.
I never say them out loud until
I've chosen the right words in my mind.

I choose to help others in need,
Even when I'd rather play.
Together we can get the work done,
So that everyone has a great day.

This is why I choose to make good decisions.
I pause to think before I act as often as I can.
It's the only way I can ensure I do the right thing
When I'm faced with an obstacle I hadn't planned.

PAUSE

I like to think about how others will feel.
And the impact of what I decide.
I make a choice that I feel confident about
So I don't feel I have to hide.

I start by thinking of the other person
Or the people I will affect.
Sometimes, I ask them how they will feel
To see if they object.

And if my decision might upset them,
I try to choose another way,
Because I never want to be the reason
Someone has a spoiled day.

I choose to stay out of danger,
To respect my body and my health.
My good decisions help me
Be super proud of myself!

I choose to think about the consequences
Of my words and actions before I react.
I will make good decisions,
In all my words and all my everyday acts.

Dear Reader,

Thank you for reading my book. I hope you enjoyed a "I Choose to Make Good Decisions." I spent fifteen years piecing together resources and ideas to help young children cope with big emotions.

So please tell me what you liked and even what you disliked. What kind of emotion should be in my next book?

I love to receive messages from my readers. Please write to me at Elizabethestradainfo@gmail.com

I would also greatly appreciate it if you could review my book.Your feedback matters a lot to me!

With love,
Elizabeth

www.ingramcontent.com/pod-product-compliance
Lightning Source LLC
Chambersburg PA
CBHW042024090426

42811CB00016B/1736